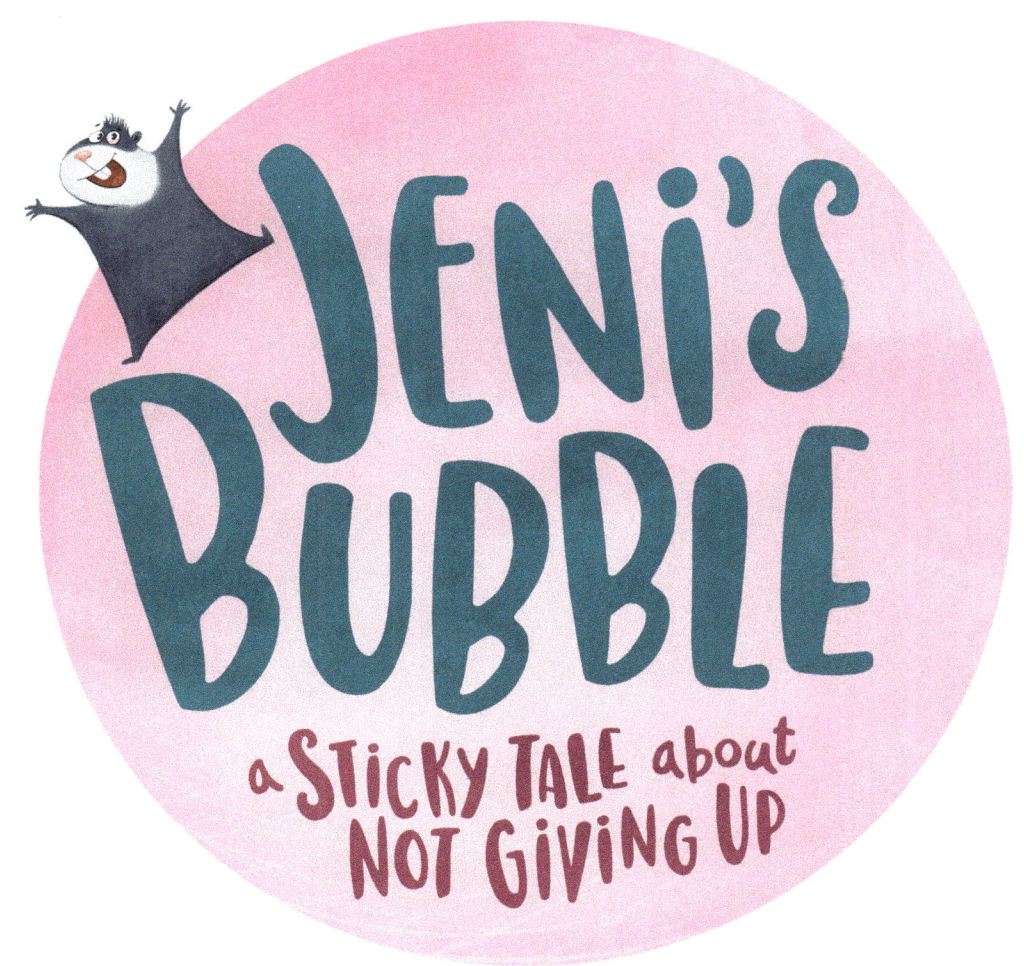

Jeni's Bubble

a Sticky Tale about Not Giving Up

by Ann-Margret Manley

illustrated by Elena Kochetova

Jeni's Bubble

Copyright © 2021 by Ann-Margret Ewald Manley
All rights reserved.
www.manleychildrensmedia.com

No part of this publication may be reproduced in
whole or in part, or stored in a retrieval system,
or transmitted in any form or by any means,
electronic, mechanical, photocopying, recording, or otherwise,
without written permission from the author or publisher.
For information regarding permission,
write to ann-margret@manleychildrensmedia.com.

Printed in the United States of America

Published by Manley Children's Media

ISBN 978-1-7374524-0-9

This book is dedicated with love to my husband and children; my sister, Jeni; my mom, Judy; and the loving memory of my grandma, Margaret. Each of you played a special part in making this decades-long dream a reality. I could not have done it without you.

Oh,
how Jeni wished
she could blow bubbles
with her gum!

It seemed
like everywhere
Jeni went,
people were
blowing
bubbles.

One day, Grandma came to visit. She hadn't even taken off her coat when Jeni jumped up and begged,

"Grandma! Will you teach me how to blow bubbles like you? The really, really BIG kind!"

"Of course I'll teach you," Grandma said with a smile.

"But it's going to take some PRACTICE."

Jeni could barely contain her excitement as she went with Grandma to the living room.

"Okay, Jeni," Grandma began. "First, you've got to stick your tongue into the gum like this."

"It helps if you wave your arms back and forth while you do it. Maybe you can skip around for a second or two."

"Stomping on my right foot and jumping around a few times are things I always do. They make a big difference. Then **blow** into the **hole** like this," Grandma said.

Jeni listened very carefully and giggled as she watched Grandma's tricks. Then it was her turn to try.

First, the gum wouldn't wrap around her tongue.

Next, it wouldn't stretch out evenly enough.

Then it got clumpy on one side and too thin on the other.

"I'm the only person
in the world
who can't blow bubbles!"
Jeni said with a pout.

Grandma simply patted Jeni on the head and handed her several packs of gum.

"Be sure to PRACTICE," Grandma reminded her.

 Practice, she did. Jeni practiced early in the morning after waking up.

She practiced during every meal she ate.

 She even practiced while she slept.

"Practice makes perfect," she encouraged herself.

Soon, Grandma came to visit again. Jeni rushed to meet her at the door.

Before Grandma could even say hi, Jeni shouted, "Grandma, I have a **surprise** for you! Please come and see! I've been waiting all day to show you what I can do!"

Jeni dragged Grandma
into the kitchen.
She dug into her pocket
and pulled out
a huge piece of gum.

"Watch, Grandma! I can blow a bubble just like you!"

Jeni said with excitement.

"I've been working so hard! You were right. I just needed practice!"

Jeni popped the gum into her mouth and chewed it up really well. Then she began to blow.

Jeni BLEW...

and BLEW...

and BLEW

some more.

Soon, the bubble covered Jeni's entire face.

"You can **stop now, honey**,"

Grandma suggested as she started to sweat.

But Jeni couldn't stop. She wanted to show Grandma that she could blow

the biggest BUBBLE there ever was.

POP

went the bubble...

all over Jeni's little face.

Ann-Margret Ewald Manley

is a former elementary school teacher. Before she got married and started a family, her love of children's books and teaching young children led her to complete a Master's degree in Reading and Language Arts at Oakland University. Ann-Margret has been married to her college sweetheart, Michael, for 32 years. She has an adult daughter and a high-school-aged son, and she lives in Fenton, Michigan, where she has raised her family for the last 25 years. JENI'S BUBBLE is Ann-Margret's first children's book. It has been a dream of hers to publish it since she originally wrote it in 1988.

Elena Kochetova
illustrator

Hi! My name is Elena and I am an illustrator. Like many of us, I look at my childhood through rose-colored glasses. For this reason, my imagination creates cute and funny characters.

I love to bring a bit of humor and naivety to the illustrations. I believe that this is the most delicate and correct way to teach and deliver emotions to our readers.

CPSIA information can be obtained
at www.ICGtesting.com
Printed in the USA
BVHW020815080821
613729BV00018B/539